TIPS FOR
NON PROFITS

a primer on communication, fundamental human needs and motivations

Gail Cassidy

Dedication

Having had the priviledge of serving on over a dozen non profits boards in my hometown, I feel qualified to laud and applaud the many volunteers who make these organizations effective and efficient.

Without the existence of these non profits, fewer students could afford to go to college, social needs of those in need would not be met, the arts would be curtailed, the beauty of the towns would lessned, and, overall, the needs of the people would not be met.

Volunteers give countless hours to fulfill the mission of their non profit organization. I congratulate them; I admire them; I encourage them to continue giving of themselves. The "specialness" of towns are a result of the dedication of these selfless volunteers.

Congratulations!!

Disclaimer and Terms of Use:

The Author and Publisher has strived to be as accurate and complete as possible in the creation of this book, notwithstanding the fact that he does not warrant or represent at any time that the contents within are accurate due to the rapidly changing nature of the Internet. While all attempts have been made to verify information provided in this publication, the Author and Publisher assume no responsibility for errors, omissions, or contrary interpretation of the subject matter herein. Any perceived slights of specific persons, peoples, or organizations are unintentional.

Printed in the United States of America, First Printing,

Tomlyn Publications
547 Shackamaxon Drive
Westfield, NJ 07090
http://www.coachability.com

TIPS FOR
NON PROFITS

a primer on communication, fundamental human needs and motivations

Table of Contents

TIPS FOR NON-PROFIT BOARDS

Non-profit organizations are in existence to make a difference in a community, state, or nation. They exist to address a need, and that is what makes being a part of the group you choose so rewarding and satisfying.

In contrast to businesses, non-profits have a different type of financial motivation. While earning money is necessary in order to exist, they use their surplus revenues differently than businesses do. Non-profits use their funds to cover their expenses, achieve their goals or expand or fulfill specific plans.

What all non-profits have in common are boards of directors, a selected group of people who are responsible for the development of policies that guide and direct their organization, including members of their staff, volunteers, and management. Having each board member "buy in" to the organization's mission can determine the success or failure of the organization.

Every non-profit has a **mission,** a statement of intent to fulfill a need that induces people to participate, donate, and be a part of the organization. It helps to carefully and clearly construct the mission statement in order to communicate with the public why you are in existence and to give volunteers and staff members something to guide their work. Staying "on mission" is a primary responsibility of each member of the board. The way the board does its work is one of the things to specify in a manual developed for each board member.

General areas to be included in a Board Manual could include topics such as: The Mission Statement, By-Laws, Strategic Plan, List of Board and Committees, New Board Member Orientation, Statement of Understanding, Job Description, Board Member Recruitment procedures, Budget, Financials, Audit, Minutes, Reports, Staff Chart.

Specific information for the formation, running, and closing of a nonprofit can be readily found on the internet. One excellent site is http://www.idealist.org/info/Nonprofits. A sidebar on their site directs the reader to additional information on a number of topics.

- Fundamentals
- The must-haves for any organization
- Mission Statements
- Board of directors
- Charter documents
- Ethics and stewardship
- Conflict of interest policies
- Running a nonprofit
- Management 101
- Strategic planning
- Finding help
- Tech tools
- Fraud! Abuse!
- Closing a nonprofit
- Financial support
- Fundraising 101
- What to consider when asking for money
- Working as a fundraiser
- Fundraising events

- Abuses in fundraising

While the structure and mission of non-profits differ one from another and may change as time progresses, some things have not changed since the beginning of civilized society; namely, fundamental human needs and motivations, and that is what this book addresses.

Board members who master the basics of fundamental human needs and motivations will be strong contributors to the success of their non-profit's existence.

Being a part of a non-profit organization is a wonderful and satisfying avocation, but it is also one that can be filled with challenges and frustrations. From my many years of public/private school and corporate training and non profit board activity, I have found the following tips to be relevant for almost all situations dealing with the public and meeting their expectations as well as the expectations of the organization.

Enjoy reading the tips. Highlight those you want to keep in the forefront of your mind. Enjoy your non profit experience. You will receive tremendous satisfaction from knowing you are in a position to make a difference in your community and in the lives of those with whom you deal. New unique ideas in your field and the individual perspectives of your peers, volunteers, members of the community, and staff members, will provide you with the gift of never-ending fond memories. You will have made a difference!

PHILOSOPHY

1. See the invisible tattoo on everyone's forehead that reads: **"PLEASE MAKE ME FEEL IMPORTANT."**

2. Find at least one happening each day with your agency to be grateful for.

3. Look for positives in opposing views.

4. Recognize the specialness of a diversity of ideas.

5. Provide an atmosphere conducive to objective decision making.

6. Be all inclusive in your decision making.

7. Remember when presenting your position that people cannot listen and absorb for extended periods of time. 20-25 minutes maximum/ break/continue.

8. Encourage input from visitors so they can be involved with your organization. Everyone has something special to offer.

9. Remind others that it is okay to be nice. It feels

good, and others are appreciative.

10. Learn the Serenity Prayer: "God, grant me the

serenity to accept the things I cannot change, courage to change the things I can and the wisdom to know the difference."

11. See" and/or "feel" your positive non profit experience before any meeting starts via positive self talk.

12. Be (or act) enthusiastic about everything you do. It's contagious; it carries over to the recipients of your comments and presentations.

13. Accept people as they are, and then provide the atmosphere and reason for them to trust this organization.

14. Learn from every colleague, every visitor, every supporter and critic.

15. Ask yourself, "Does it really matter?"

16. Being right does not always work, e.g., Here lies the body of William Jay, who died maintaining his right of way. He was right, dead right as he sped along, but he's just as dead as if he were wrong.

17. HAVE FUN!

ATTITUDE

18. Park your ego at the door; it hinders relationships.

19. Give your audience a reason to check their negative attitudes at the door also.

20. Know that people "mirror" you. They reflect what they see, hear, and feel from you.

21. Shake things up. Make changes. "If you always do what you have always done, you'll always get what you've always got."

22. Show your peers through your own example the effectiveness of having a great attitude is.

23. Be patient.

24. Positive attitudes are catching.

25. Show respect to get respect.

26. Know that attitude is a choice everyone makes every day.

27. Explain that people cannot help what happens to them, but they are **always** in charge of their responses.

28. Remember, there is a pause between stimulus

and response. Choose your response carefully.

29. If feeling discouraged, ask yourself why you are **choosing** this emotion.

30. Know that attitude is the steering mechanism of the brain. Body language can lead to attitude.

31. Have your peers practice changing their attitudes by sitting or standing straight, with their heads up, and a smile on their faces. It does work!

32. Know that it is the attitude of our hearts and minds that shape who we are, how we live, and how we treat others.

33. Through your response to criticism you can disarm your critics by recognizing a positive in some aspect of their opinion, their presentation, or their impact on the audience.

34. Success is feeling good about yourself every single day. That is attitude.

35. Know that true power is knowing that you can control your attitude at all times. Disagreement with your point of view cannot nettle you unless you allow it to.

HUMAN RELATIONS

36. Treat every critic as if he or she were a friend.

37. Never talk down to anyone.

38. Find what is significant about every decision to be made and how it will affect all groups.

39. **SMILE.** It warms a room.

40. Use tact when responding to a challenging person. The rewards outweigh "being right."

41. Know that your position is not bolstered by any critic who feels your negativity.

42. Be 100% fair at all times--no exceptions.

43. Keep in mind that perception is reality--yours and your critics'.

44. Treat every person as you wish to be treated.

45. Understand that no one **wants** to be wrong.

46. **Everyone desperately wants to feel special.**

47. Remember that people gravitate toward things that are pleasurable and avoid things that are painful. Make dealing with your organization a pleasurable experience.

48. **LISTENING** is the greatest compliment.

49. Try to understand before being understood.

50. Be genuinely appreciative of all comments, positive and/or negative.

51. Begin corrective action with sincere and honest recognition of what has been done correctly.

52. Never embarrass a critic. Allow the critic to save face.

53. Use encouragement. Make the error seem easy to correct.

54. Don't be afraid to admit your mistakes. It will make you appear more human.

55. Show respect for every person's opinion.

56. Challenge your peers, volunteers, and staff to be the best that they can be.

57. Make **SINCERITY** your No. 1 priority.

COMMUNICATION

58. Set standards in your organization and share them with your audience.

59. Explain the purpose and importance of what you are making a decision on. Give them reasons for the change(s). Personalize it.

60. Set high expectations. Remember the story of the new teacher who thought the locker list from 140-160 was the list of IQ's in her class and she treated them accordingly, and they performed accordingly. Your situation dealing with people is no different.

61. Know that 55% of all messages comes from the body. Notice how you can tell your special someone is in a bad mood without any words being spoken. Your audience can "read" you also.

62. Know that 38% of the message comes from the voice: inflection, intonation, pitch, speed, e.g., "I didn't say he stole the exam." Seven words--seven meanings.

63. Know, you **cannot NOT** communicate.

64. Recognize that we don't all see the same thing when looking at the same thing. This is especially

important in decision making.

65. Know also that we don't all hear the same things even when listening to the same words.

66. Control your thoughts; your feelings come from your thoughts; therefore, you can also control your feelings! Choice is control.

67. Teach those whom you encounter to take responsibility for what they say and how they say it.

68. Listen for the message, yet know that body language can be interpreted as only a clue to the meaning of the message, e.g., arms crossed in front of chest could mean blocking you or could mean person is actually cold or comfortable.

69. Learn to lead rather than to try and overcome resistance.

70. Communicate your enthusiasm through your body and voice.

71. "One who is too insistent on his own views, find few to agree with him." -Lao-Tze

72. **Speak with a warm heart.**

SELF ESTEEM

73. Know that a person with high self-esteem does not need to find fault with others and can be understanding of the views of others.

74. Remember that people find fault with others when they feel threatened, consciously or unconsciously.

75. Know that self-esteem is not noisy conceit. It is a quiet sense of self-respect, a feeling of self-worth. Conceit is whitewash to cover low self-esteem.

76. Remember, people have two basic needs: to know they are **lovable** and **worthwhile**.

77. Remember, it is a person's feeling about being respected or not respected that affects how s/he will behave and perform.

78. Helping your organization's board members to believe in themselves is the key to successful decision making.

79. Know that your words have power to affect a person's self-esteem.

80. Each person values himself to the degree s/he has been valued.

81. Words are less important in their affect on self-esteem than the judgments that accompany them.

82. The attitude of others toward a person's capacities are more important than his possession of particular traits.

83. Braggarts are asking for positive reflections; otherwise, they would not need to brag.

84. Masks are worn to hide the "worthless me."

85. Low self-esteem is tied to impossible demands on the self.

86. A person's own self-acceptance frees him or her to focus on the challenge, unencumbered by inner needs.

87. The single most important ingredient in an effective working relationship is honesty.

88. Ask this: "If I were to treat my friends as I treat my critics, how many friends would I have left?"

89. Avoid mixed messages. Be clear in your statements of expectations.

RESPECTFULNESS

90.   Tolerate no disrespect.

91.   Be consistent in enforcing rules.

92.   Set boundaries.

93.   Find opportunities for your peers to improve the quality of his/her work.

94.   Differientate between the action and the person.

95.   Uncover and address, when possible, the reasons for the person's poor performance.

96.   Make sure people have the skills to succeed.

97.   Focus, as often as possible, on what is right rather than what is wrong.

98.   Give plenty of recognition for the unique gifts of each person.

99.   Teach people to know they have power in the present moment to change their thoughts, feelings, and attitude about the past.

100.   Remind people to take control of their lives by focusing on the present.

101. Remove the word "try" from co-workers' vocabulary. Have them "try" to pick up a pencil. Either they do or they don't.

102. Work with challenging peers to find the lesson or value in unacceptable situations.

103. Make sure people know they have choices in spite of their past experiences.

104. Set an example by turning any problem into a learning opportunity.

105. Make sure issues are clear to every person in a decision-making position.

106. Approach problematic board and audience members with relaxed confidence.

107. Being a model for people to follow provides them with a picture of what appropriate behavior looks like.

108. Respond thoughtfully to challenging and/or problem situations--avoid making judgments.

109. To save hours of useless discussion, teach problem solving to every board member:

   a. State the problem

   b. Look for causes of the problem

   c. Brainstorm solutions

d. Choose the best one

The last three steps are time wasters if the problem has not been clearly stated.

110. Encourage members to see beyond their own point of view.

111. Encourage habits of thought conducive to growth in understanding others, to think outside the box.

112. Recognize that there is no one interpretation of a situation.

113. Everyone is a product of his/her experiences which colors all decisions made.

TREASURE TIPS

114. Know that you too are special.

115. Enjoy every day and every challenge.

116. Make corrections by citing two positives for every negative.

117. Make decisions relevant to the best interests of those affected.

118. Be alert to teachable moments for peers and audience.

119. Show lively enthusiasm!

120. Create an atmosphere of fun.

121. Build on successes.

122. Create a routine with varied activities.

123. Turn all people on to your cause.

124. Encourage people to visualize doing well.

125. Have a relaxed environment.

126. Make every active participant feel important.

127. Give one instruction at a time.

128. Give volunteers and staff opportunities to succeed.

129. Provide a safe atmosphere.

130. Validate your peers frequently.

131. Understand peoples' learning modalities, e.g., visual, kinesthetic, auditory.

132. Recognize the positive value of peer pressure in learning.

133. Recognize that most people are on a quest for identity and some sense of personal power.

134. Above all, enjoy each day--your peers are more likely to also. You are the mirror.

TIPS FOR ADMINISTRATORS

- Validate your employees on a regular basis, not just during a special review.

- Tell staff members specifically what you like about what they are doing. They will work harder to earn that recognition again in the future.

- Encourage board members and staff to strive for excellence. "We are what we repeatedly do. Excellence, then, is not an act but a habit." -Aristotle.

- Encourage staff members to align their goals with their values. Conflict arises when the two are in conflict.

- Expect the best from your staff. People live up to expectations.

- Always abide by the golden rule: "Do unto others as you would have them do unto you."

- Involve as many employees as you can in your organization's activities. Those who participant feel more a part of the "family."

- Always always be fair.

- Avoid being judgmental.

- Treat your staff to something special, e.g., bagels. Let them know you care.

- Encourage staff to use their powers of observation and logic. Successful staff members see details and discover principles that others do not.

- Encourage and enable staff members to continually grow. Complacency breeds stagnation.

- Make your staff proud to be a part of your "family."

TIPS FOR ALL STAFF

- Work towards feeling good about yourself. It is man's highest goal.

- Always do what you feel is right or true.

- Your actions reveal your values.

- Your thought is the most powerful force in your universe. "Nothing is either good or bad but thinking makes it so." -Shakespeare.

- Whatever you dwell on expands.

- Work toward goals that cause you to feel a sense of mastery.

- Write a list of everything you have accomplished or have been recognized for in your life. Add to it whenever you think of something new. Read it when the going gets tough.

- Have a clear sense of purpose in life.

- Clarify your goals and focus on them

- Be a risk taker. Step outside your comfort zone. Try something new.

- Polish your people skills.

- Hone your communications skills.

- Take excellent care of yourself.

- Positive expectations are the single, most outwardly identifiable, characteristics all successful people possess.

- Your reality is what you make it to be.

- You can train yourself to think more positively by training yourself to choose what you pay attention to and what you say about it, both to yourself and others. "We know what we are but know not what we may be." -Shakespeare.

- Whatever you believe, picture in your mind, and think about most of the time, you eventually will bring into reality.

- Your self-image is the most dominant factor that affects everything you attempt to do.

- Nothing is more exciting than the realization that you can accomplish anything you really want that is consistent with your unique mix of natural talents and abilities.

TEN WAYS TO ENHANCE YOUR ORGANIZATION'S EFFECTIVENESS

GOALS: Create community through the sharing of ideas; develop leadership; promote excellence, and prepare volunteers to the best of their abilities.

1. Give each member of your agency a copy of *Tips for Non-Profits*.

2. Personalize the booklets with your logo.

3. Have copies available for guests and visitors.

4. Have copies of the booklet available in your main office for members of the public to peruse.

5. Use the ideas in the booklet for discussion with committees.

6. Encourage volunteers and staff to use these concepts for researching policy changes.

7. Ask members to add to the lists.

8. Use individual lists as topics for general discussion. Find areas of agreement and disagreement.

9. Use these principles as the basis for your agency's standards.

10. Expand the consciousness of board members, volunteers, staff and administrators through the discussion of these concepts.

WORTHY QUOTES

- Assume a virtue, if you have it not. - Shakespeare.

- Act enthusiastic and you'll be enthusiastic. -Carnegie.

- Begin to be now what you will be hereafter. - St. Jerome. Repetition is the mother of skill.

- It is not the place, nor the condition, but the mind alone that can make any one happy or miserable. - L Estrange.

- Beliefs have the power to create and the power to destroy. - Robbins.

- Nothing is more likely to help a person overcome or endure troubles than the consciousness of having a task in life. - Frankl.

- When the student is ready, the teacher will appear. - Zen proverb.

- The ancestor to every action is a thought. -Emerson.

- Imagination is more important than knowledge. -Albert Einstein.

- Things do not change; we change. -Thoreau.

- Change your thoughts and you change your world. - Norman Vincent Peale.

- Great men are those who see that thoughts rule the world. - Emerson.

- Nothing has any power over me other than that which I give it through my conscious thoughts. -Anthony Robbins.

- The greatest discovery of my generation is that human beings can alter their lives by altering their attitudes of mind.
  - William James.

- You are what you choose today. -Dyer.

- To waken interest and kindle enthusiasm is the sure way to teach easily and successfully. - Tyron Edwards.

- The only limits you have are the limits you believe. -Wayne Dyer.

- Anything we fail to reinforce will eventually dissipate.
  - Robbins.

- Patience is the companion of wisdom. -Augustine.

- The more he gives to others, the more he possesses of his own. -Lao-Tze.

- Vision is the art of seeing things invisible. -Swift.

- What the mind can conceive and believe, it can achieve.
  – Napoleon Hill.

- Believing is seeing. -Dyer.

- A man there was, and they called him mad; the more he gave, the more he had. -Bunyan

- What I gave, I have; what I spent, I had; what I kept, I lost.
  - Old Epitaph

- To give away money is an easy matter and in any man's power. But to decide to whom to give it and how large and when, and for what purpose and how, is neither in every man's power nor an easy matter. - Aristotle

- Even the smallest person in the world can change the course of the universe. - JRR Tolkien (Lord of the Rings)

- Difficult things we do quickly. The impossible takes a little longer. - David Ben-Gurion

- I've always respected those who tried to change the world for the better, rather than just complain about it.
  - Michael Bloomberg

- I resolved to stop accumulating and begin the infinitely more serious and difficult task of wise distribution.
  - Andrew Carnegie

- Wealth is not to feed our egos, but to feed the hungry and to help people help themselves. - Andrew Carnegie

- We make a living by what we get, we make a life by what we give. - Winston Churchill

- The value of a man resides in what he gives and not in what he is capable of receiving. - Albert Einstein

- It is every man's obligation to put back into the world at least the equivalent of what he takes out of it. - Albert Einstein

- How wonderful it is that nobody needs to wait a single moment before starting to improve the world. - Anne Frank

- I would rather have it said, 'He lived usefully,' than, 'He died rich.' - Benjamin Franklin

- If you want to change the world, be that change.
  - Mohandas Gandhi

- Helping people doesn't have to be an unsound financial strategy. - Melinda Gates

- Life is a loan that we must return one day, and it is not interest free. The interest we pay is to make the world a little better than when we entered. - Eliezer Jaffe

- If a free society cannot help the many who are poor, it cannot save the few who are rich. - John F. Kennedy

- Every man must decide whether he will walk in the creative light of altruism or the darkness of destructive selfishness. This is the judgement. Life's persistent and most urgent question is "What are you doing for others?" - Martin Luther King Jr.

- Philanthropy is commendable, but it must not cause the philanthropist to overlook the circumstances of economic injustice which make philanthropy necessary.
  - Martin Luther King, Jr.

- Think of giving not only as a duty but as a privilege.
  - John D. Rockefeller

- I was trained from the beginning to work, to save, and to give. - John D. Rockefeller, Jr.

- It's not just about being able to write a check. It's being able to touch somebody's life. -Oprah Winfrey

- Paul Schervish: Donors used to support nonprofits to help them acheive their mission. Now we support nonprofits so that they can help us achieve our personal mission.

- Serious philanthropy is serious work.

- An essential element of philanthropy is measurement.

- Philanthropy is not a matter of doing the right thing; it is a matter of doing the right thing for you.

- In philanthropy, the choices are not between right and wrong, but between right and right.

- In philanthropy you can't just "go for it."

- [Organizations:] Follow your mission; don't follow the money. If you follow the mission, money will come. If you follow the money, the mission can get lost somewhere behind you.

- [When joining of Board of Directors:] A donor has to rely on the strength of ideas, not the amount of the gift.

- Michael Hammer: You can't improve what you can't measure.

- The nonprofit realm lacks the bottom-line measure of for-profits, but that doesn't mean it lacks any measures at all.

- Good evaluation can attract donors.

- By deciding what it is that we seek to measure, we learn what it is we most strongly value.

Jim Collins – Good to Great and the Social Sectors

- We must reject the idea — well-intentioned, but dead wrong — that the primary path to greatness in the social sectors is to become "more like a business."

- In business, money is both an input and an output. In the social sectors, money is only an input, and not a measure of greatness.

- The basic idea is still the same: separate inputs from outputs, and hold yourself accountable for progress in outputs, even if those outputs defy measurement.

- It really doesn't matter whether you can quantify your results. What matters is that you rigorously assemble evidence — quantitative or qualitative — to track your progress.

- Greatness is an inherently dynamic process, not an end point.

- Social sectors leaders only appear less decisive than business leaders to those who fail to grasp the complex governance and diffuse power structures. (pg 10)

- Ironic: Social sector organizations increasingly look to business for leadership models and talent, yet I suspect we will find more true leadership in social sectors that the business sector.

- The practice of leadership is not the exercise of power.

- True leadership only exists if people follow when they have the freedom not to.

- Peter Drucker: The foundation for doing good is doing well.

- In social sectors, unfortunately, there is no guarantee between exceptional results an sustained access to resources.

- Key link in the social sectors is brand reputation so that potential supporters believe not only in your mission, but in your capacity to deliver on that mission.

- Great business corporations share more in common with great social sector organizations than they share with mediocre businesses.

- Greatness is not a function of circumstance. Greatness, it turns out, is largely a matter of conscious choice, and discipline.

[Above quotes from Shuey Fogel, The Nonprofit Banker (www.nonprofitbanker.com) A nonprofit professional turned banking specialist shares conversations, articles, and experiences.]

As the sword of the best tempered metal is most flexible, so the truly generous are most pliant and courteous in their behavior to others.   -Fuller

www.ingramcontent.com/pod-product-compliance
Lightning Source LLC
Chambersburg PA
CBHW070518290526
45790CB00003B/1255